BASEBALL

ENGAGEMENT CALENDAR 1995

Based on an Illustrated History
by GEOFFREY C. WARD and KEN BURNS

Alfred A. Knopf New York

THIS IS A BORZOI BOOK
PUBLISHED BY ALFRED A. KNOPF, INC.

Cover photograph: A small-town New Hampshire club celebrates
the Fourth of July, about 1890. Courtesy of Dennis Goldstein, Atlanta, Georgia
Cover design by Archie Ferguson
Calendar design by Virginia Tan

ISBN 0-679-75386-9

First Edition

26
MONDAY

27
TUESDAY

28
WEDNESDAY

29
THURSDAY

30
FRIDAY

31
SATURDAY

NEW YEAR'S DAY

1
SUNDAY

DECEMBER 1994 / JANUARY 1995

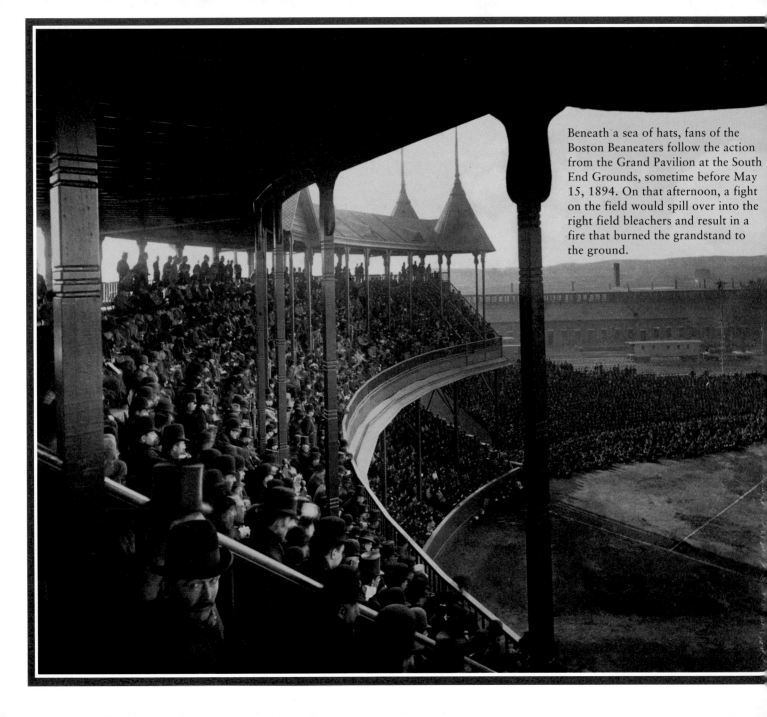

Beneath a sea of hats, fans of the Boston Beaneaters follow the action from the Grand Pavilion at the South End Grounds, sometime before May 15, 1894. On that afternoon, a fight on the field would spill over into the right field bleachers and result in a fire that burned the grandstand to the ground.

2
MONDAY

3
TUESDAY

4
WEDNESDAY

5
THURSDAY

6
FRIDAY

7
SATURDAY

8
SUNDAY

Hat in hand, a Union prisoner takes off for second in a game played under
Confederate guard at Salisbury, North Carolina, during the Civil War.

9
MONDAY

10
TUESDAY

11
WEDNESDAY

12
THURSDAY

13
FRIDAY

14
SATURDAY

15
SUNDAY

THE NATIONAL GAME. THREE "OUTS" AND ONE "RUN".
ABRAHAM WINNING THE BALL.

The national pastime had already become a universally understood metaphor when Currier & Ives published this cartoon marking batter Abraham Lincoln's 1860 presidential election victory over (left to right) John Bell, Stephen A. Douglas, and John Breckinridge.

MARTIN LUTHER KING, JR.'S BIRTHDAY *observed*

16
MONDAY

17
TUESDAY

18
WEDNESDAY

19
THURSDAY

20
FRIDAY

21
SATURDAY

22
SUNDAY

WESTERN BLOOMER GIRLS
ST AUGUSTINE, FLA.

A traveling women's team, photographed sometime after the century's turn. Future Boston pitching star Smokey Joe Wood (far right) was a special added attraction.

23
MONDAY

24
TUESDAY

25
WEDNESDAY

26
THURSDAY

27
FRIDAY

28
SATURDAY

29
SUNDAY

JANUARY 1995

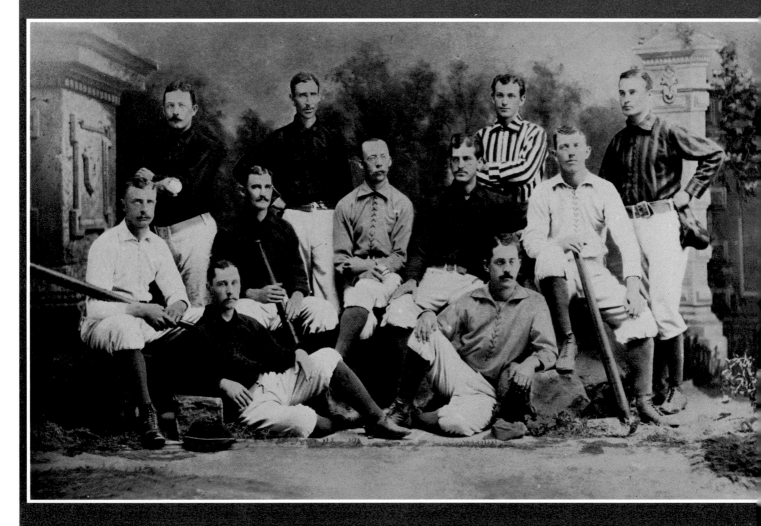

A hand-tinted photograph of Albert Spalding's Cincinnati Reds, uniformed as he wished every team would be, with each position denoted by a different colored cap and silk jersey. In the back row (left to right) stand the relief pitcher, center fielder, first baseman, and second baseman. Seated are the third baseman, catcher, pitcher, shortstop, and left fielder. At the bottom are the utility man and the right fielder. The experiment—which, at Spalding's insistence, was tried in 1882 by every major league club—was mercifully ended in June.

30
MONDAY

31
TUESDAY

1
WEDNESDAY

2
THURSDAY

GROUNDHOG DAY

3
FRIDAY

4
SATURDAY

5
SUNDAY

A Mother Hubbard team—men playing in women's clothing—somewhere in Kansas, 1895

6
MONDAY

7
TUESDAY

8
WEDNESDAY

9
THURSDAY

10
FRIDAY

11
SATURDAY

12
SUNDAY

FEBRUARY 1995

Boston fans swarm over the Huntington Avenue Grounds before the first game of the very first World Series, between the Pilgrims of the brand-new American League, and the National League Pittsburgh Pirates, October 1, 1903.

13
MONDAY

14
TUESDAY

VALENTINE'S DAY

15
WEDNESDAY

16
THURSDAY

17
FRIDAY

18
SATURDAY

19
SUNDAY

Hawking scorecards at Chicago's South Side Park, home of the White Sox from 1901 to 1910

20
MONDAY

PRESIDENTS' DAY
GEORGE WASHINGTON'S BIRTHDAY *observed*

21
TUESDAY

22
WEDNESDAY

23
THURSDAY

24
FRIDAY

25
SATURDAY

26
SUNDAY

The hands of Honus Wagner

27
MONDAY

28
TUESDAY

ASH WEDNESDAY

1
WEDNESDAY

2
THURSDAY

3
FRIDAY

4
SATURDAY

5
SUNDAY

Alta Weiss was a doctor's daughter from Ragersville, Ohio, who began to pitch for boys' teams at the age of fourteen. At sixteen she joined a men's semiprofessional team, th nearby Vermilion Independents. Her basebal skills were good enough to put her through medical school. Even after she began to practice as a physician, she continued to play off and on into the 1920s.

6
MONDAY

7
TUESDAY

8
WEDNESDAY

9
THURSDAY

10
FRIDAY

11
SATURDAY

12
SUNDAY

MARCH 1995

"When I began playing," Cobb remembered, "baseball was as gentlemanly as a kick in the crotch."

13
MONDAY

COMMONWEALTH DAY (*Canada*)

14
TUESDAY

15
WEDNESDAY

16
THURSDAY

17
FRIDAY

ST. PATRICK'S DAY

18
SATURDAY

19
SUNDAY

MARCH 1995

The barnstorming Page Fence Giants from Adrian, Michigan, stop along the road long enough to pose with rolls of their white sponsor's products; shortly after this photograph was made, the team's best players moved to Chicago and became the Columbia Giants. Charlie Grant, the player John McGraw tried to slip into the big leagues by claiming he was an Indian, sits atop the bale at the left.

27
MONDAY

28
TUESDAY

29
WEDNESDAY

30
THURSDAY

31
FRIDAY

1
SATURDAY

DAYLIGHT SAVING TIME BEGINS
2
SUNDAY

TAKE ME OUT TO THE BALL GAME

One day in 1908, a vaudeville entertainer named Jack Norworth boarded a Manhattan elevated train and saw an advertisement that read, "Baseball Today—Polo Grounds." Norworth was looking for new material. He had never been to a professional game, but by the time he reached his stop he had scribbled out the lyrics for a song about baseball. And he asked a friend, Albert Von Tilzer—who had also never seen a game—to write the melody. When Norworth introduced the song in his act at the Amphion Theater in Brooklyn, it fell flat, but it was soon a nationwide hit nonetheless, helped b song-slides that encouraged nickelodeon audiences to sing along. It became baseball anthem.

Katie Casey was baseball mad,
had the fever and had it bad;
Just to root for the hometown crew,
ev'ry sou—Katie blew.

On a Saturday, her young beau called to see if she'd like to go,
To see a show but Miss Kate said, "No,
I'll tell you what you can do":

Take me out to the ball game,
Take me out with the crowd.

Buy me some peanuts
And Cracker Jack,
I don't care if I never get back,

Let me root, root, root,
for the home team,
If they don't win it's a shame—

For it's one, two, three strikes
you're out
At the old ball game.

3
MONDAY

4
TUESDAY

5
WEDNESDAY

6
THURSDAY

7
FRIDAY

8
SATURDAY

9
SUNDAY

PALM SUNDAY

William Howard Taft in action on opening day

10
MONDAY

11
TUESDAY

12
WEDNESDAY

13
THURSDAY

14
FRIDAY

GOOD FRIDAY

15
SATURDAY

PASSOVER

16
SUNDAY

EASTER

The Play-O-Graph recording the 1912 World Series

17
MONDAY

18
TUESDAY

19
WEDNESDAY

20
THURSDAY

21
FRIDAY

22
SATURDAY

23
SUNDAY

APRIL 1995

Dodgers' rookie center fielder Casey Stengel

24
MONDAY

25
TUESDAY

26
WEDNESDAY

27
THURSDAY

28
FRIDAY

29
SATURDAY

30
SUNDAY

The athletic assistant secretary of the navy, Franklin Delano Roosevelt, leads the
Washington Senators onto the field in a demonstration of preparedness for the
war effort, 1917.

1
MONDAY

2
TUESDAY

3
WEDNESDAY

4
THURSDAY

5
FRIDAY

6
SATURDAY

7
SUNDAY

Joe Jackson at bat: "I decided to pick out the greatest hitter to watch and study," Babe Ruth would say, "and Jackson was good enough for me."

15
MONDAY

16
TUESDAY

17
WEDNESDAY

18
THURSDAY

19
FRIDAY

20
SATURDAY

21
SUNDAY

MAY 1995

In the second game of the 1919 series, White Sox third baseman Buck Weaver—who knew of the plot to throw the championship and did not report it but played as hard as he could to win—is tagged out by Cincinnati catcher Bill Rariden.

VICTORIA DAY (*Canada*)

22
MONDAY

23
TUESDAY

24
WEDNESDAY

25
THURSDAY

26
FRIDAY

27
SATURDAY

28
SUNDAY

MAY 1995

A crowd in New York's Times Square follows 1919 series action on an automated scoreboard linked to the distant ballpark by telegraph.

5
MONDAY

6
TUESDAY

7
WEDNESDAY

8
THURSDAY

9
FRIDAY

10
SATURDAY

11
SUNDAY

JUNE 1995

EAST-WEST-1939.
(2)   (4)   COMISKEY PARK-CHICAGO

ATTENDANCE-40,000

Negro League All-Stars at the 1939 East-West game. Standing (left to right): Buck Leonard, Willie Wells, Rudy Fernandez, Sammy Hughes, George Scales, Mule Suttles, Pat Patterson, Josh Gibson, Bill Wright, Roy Partlow. Kneeling: Bill Byrd, Leon Day, Bill Holland, Cando Lopez, Goose Curry, Red Parnell

12
MONDAY

13
TUESDAY

14
WEDNESDAY

FLAG DAY

15
THURSDAY

16
FRIDAY

17
SATURDAY

18
SUNDAY

FATHER'S DAY

JUNE 1995

Josh Gibson heads for home at Washington's Griffith Stadium, where
Homestead Gray games were played when the Senators were away.

19
MONDAY

20
TUESDAY

21
WEDNESDAY

SUMMER SOLSTICE

22
THURSDAY

23
FRIDAY

24
SATURDAY

25
SUNDAY

The strange spectacle of uncut hair may have initially pulled crowds out to see the barnstorming House of David teams, but brilliant ball handling kept them coming back for more, year after year.

26
MONDAY

27
TUESDAY

28
WEDNESDAY

29
THURSDAY

30
FRIDAY

1
SATURDAY

CANADA DAY (*Canada*)

2
SUNDAY

"Listen," said Satchel Paige, "if I had to do it over again, I would. I had more fun and seen more places with less money than if I was a Rockefeller." Here the player, who was as good at self-promotion as he was at strikeouts, stands with the private plane in which he winged his way from game to game during the early 1940s.

10
MONDAY

11
TUESDAY

12
WEDNESDAY

13
THURSDAY

14
FRIDAY

15
SATURDAY

16
SUNDAY

Baseball in paradise: The 1927 Cuban Stars (left to right)—Pablo Mesa, Oscar Charleston, Alejandro (Walla Walla) Olms, and Jose Rodriguez

17
MONDAY

18
TUESDAY

19
WEDNESDAY

20
THURSDAY

21
FRIDAY

22
SATURDAY

23
SUNDAY

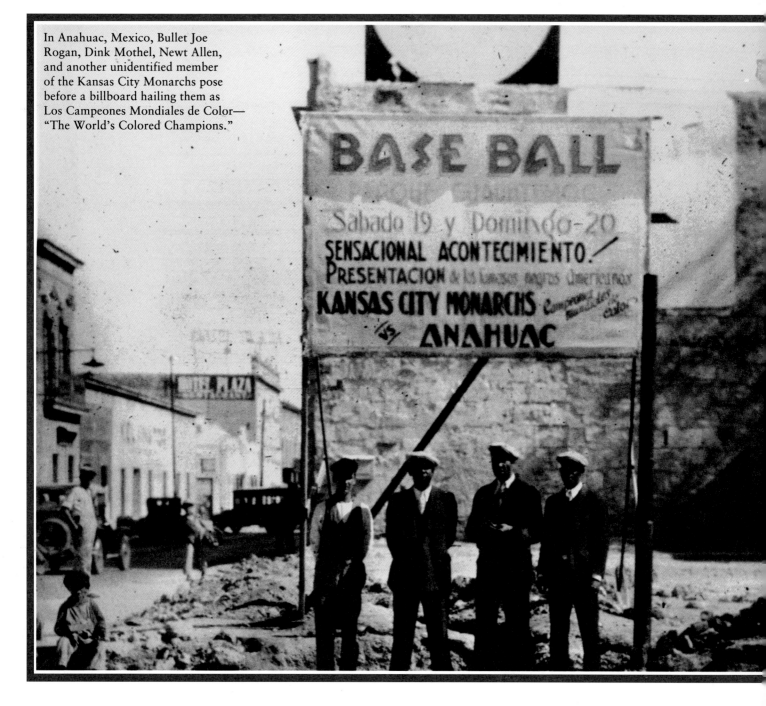

In Anahuac, Mexico, Bullet Joe Rogan, Dink Mothel, Newt Allen, and another unidentified member of the Kansas City Monarchs pose before a billboard hailing them as Los Campeones Mondiales de Color— "The World's Colored Champions."

24
MONDAY

25
TUESDAY

26
WEDNESDAY

27
THURSDAY

28
FRIDAY

29
SATURDAY

30
SUNDAY

JULY 1995

Ebbets Field, home of the Brooklyn Dodgers

31
MONDAY

1
TUESDAY

2
WEDNESDAY

3
THURSDAY

4
FRIDAY

5
SATURDAY

6
SUNDAY

Everything anyone could ever want to know about baseball. Izzy Goodman and his newsstand in Louisville, Kentucky, photographed in 19

14
MONDAY

15
TUESDAY

16
WEDNESDAY

17
THURSDAY

18
FRIDAY

19
SATURDAY

20
SUNDAY

Players in the All-American Girls Professional Baseball League in training at
Opa-Locka, Florida

21
MONDAY

22
TUESDAY

23
WEDNESDAY

24
THURSDAY

25
FRIDAY

26
SATURDAY

27
SUNDAY

Sailors take in a game at Ebbets Field during World War II.

28
MONDAY

29
TUESDAY

30
WEDNESDAY

31
THURSDAY

1
FRIDAY

2
SATURDAY

3
SUNDAY

AUGUST / SEPTEMBER 1995

Past and present linked: as the scoreboard at Riverfront Stadium salutes Pete Rose's feat,
Ty Cobb seems to return to life as well

11
MONDAY

12
TUESDAY

13
WEDNESDAY

14
THURSDAY

15
FRIDAY

16
SATURDAY

17
SUNDAY

SEPTEMBER 1995

Baseball enters the television age: the broadcaster at the microphone is
former St. Louis pitching star Dizzy Dean.

18
MONDAY

19
TUESDAY

20
WEDNESDAY

21
THURSDAY

22
FRIDAY

AUTUMNAL EQUINOX

23
SATURDAY

24
SUNDAY

GREATER MUSKEGON GIRLS PROFESSIONAL BALL CLUB

MUSKEGON LASSIES

21503

OFFICIAL

10¢

SCORE CARD

A-A
GBBL

"Watch the girls play ball"

All American Girls
PROFESSIONAL BALL LEAGUE
MARSH FIELD

Program cover for the
Muskegon Lassies

25
MONDAY

ROSH HASHANAH

26
TUESDAY

27
WEDNESDAY

28
THURSDAY

29
FRIDAY

30
SATURDAY

1
SUNDAY

Amateur baseball
league, Spencer,
Massachusetts, 1980

9
MONDAY

COLUMBUS DAY *observed*
THANKSGIVING DAY (*Canada*)

10
TUESDAY

11
WEDNESDAY

12
THURSDAY

13
FRIDAY

14
SATURDAY

15
SUNDAY

OCTOBER 1995

Grounded: the Brooklyn team plane before its regular passengers
moved to California

23
MONDAY

24
TUESDAY

25
WEDNESDAY

26
THURSDAY

27
FRIDAY

28
SATURDAY

DAYLIGHT SAVING TIME ENDS

29
SUNDAY

Pittsburgh Pirates, spring training, Bradenton, Florida, 1991

30
MONDAY

31
TUESDAY

HALLOWEEN

1
WEDNESDAY

2
THURSDAY

3
FRIDAY

4
SATURDAY

5
SUNDAY

Bat day at Yankee Stadium, 1965

6 MONDAY

7 TUESDAY

ELECTION DAY

8 WEDNESDAY

9 THURSDAY

10 FRIDAY

11 SATURDAY

VETERANS DAY
REMEMBRANCE DAY (*Canada*)

12 SUNDAY

Paradise paved: Dodger Stadium, built beside the Elysian Parkway

13
MONDAY

14
TUESDAY

15
WEDNESDAY

16
THURSDAY

17
FRIDAY

18
SATURDAY

19
SUNDAY

NOVEMBER 1995

The New York Mets and Chicago Cubs scrambling for first place in the 1969 pennant race

20 MONDAY

21 TUESDAY

22 WEDNESDAY

THANKSGIVING DAY

23 THURSDAY

24 FRIDAY

25 SATURDAY

26 SUNDAY

Little League championship play

27
MONDAY

28
TUESDAY

29
WEDNESDAY

30
THURSDAY

1
FRIDAY

2
SATURDAY

3
SUNDAY

NOVEMBER / DECEMBER 1995

George Steinbrenner rising over Yankee Stadium

4
ONDAY

5
UESDAY

6
DNESDAY

7
URSDAY

8
RIDAY

9
TURDAY

10
UNDAY

DECEMBER 1995

The Toronto Blue Jays win the World Series in 1993.

11
MONDAY

12
TUESDAY

13
WEDNESDAY

14
THURSDAY

15
FRIDAY

16
SATURDAY

17
SUNDAY

In the shadow of some of history's most dispiriting Christmas decorations, Babe Ruth (center) helps his look-alike father tend bar in 1915 or 1916.

18
MONDAY

CHANUKAH BEGINS

19
TUESDAY

20
WEDNESDAY

21
THURSDAY

22
FRIDAY

WINTER SOLSTICE

23
SATURDAY

24
SUNDAY

Fenway at twilight

25
MONDAY

CHRISTMAS DAY

26
TUESDAY

BOXING DAY (*Canada*)

27
WEDNESDAY

28
THURSDAY

29
FRIDAY

30
SATURDAY

31
SUNDAY

DECEMBER 1995

1994

JANUARY
```
 S  M  T  W  T  F  S
                   1
 2  3  4  5  6  7  8
 9 10 11 12 13 14 15
16 17 18 19 20 21 22
23 24 25 26 27 28 29
30 31
```

FEBRUARY
```
 S  M  T  W  T  F  S
       1  2  3  4  5
 6  7  8  9 10 11 12
13 14 15 16 17 18 19
20 21 22 23 24 25 26
27 28
```

MARCH
```
 S  M  T  W  T  F  S
       1  2  3  4  5
 6  7  8  9 10 11 12
13 14 15 16 17 18 19
20 21 22 23 24 25 26
27 28 29 30 31
```

APRIL
```
 S  M  T  W  T  F  S
                1  2
 3  4  5  6  7  8  9
10 11 12 13 14 15 16
17 18 19 20 21 22 23
24 25 26 27 28 29 30
```

MAY
```
 S  M  T  W  T  F  S
 1  2  3  4  5  6  7
 8  9 10 11 12 13 14
15 16 17 18 19 20 21
22 23 24 25 26 27 28
29 30 31
```

JUNE
```
 S  M  T  W  T  F  S
          1  2  3  4
 5  6  7  8  9 10 11
12 13 14 15 16 17 18
19 20 21 22 23 24 25
26 27 28 29 30
```

JULY
```
 S  M  T  W  T  F  S
                1  2
 3  4  5  6  7  8  9
10 11 12 13 14 15 16
17 18 19 20 21 22 23
24 25 26 27 28 29 30
31
```

AUGUST
```
 S  M  T  W  T  F  S
    1  2  3  4  5  6
 7  8  9 10 11 12 13
14 15 16 17 18 19 20
21 22 23 24 25 26 27
28 29 30 31
```

SEPTEMBER
```
 S  M  T  W  T  F  S
             1  2  3
 4  5  6  7  8  9 10
11 12 13 14 15 16 17
18 19 20 21 22 23 24
25 26 27 28 29 30
```

OCTOBER
```
 S  M  T  W  T  F  S
                   1
 2  3  4  5  6  7  8
 9 10 11 12 13 14 15
16 17 18 19 20 21 22
23 24 25 26 27 28 29
30 31
```

NOVEMBER
```
 S  M  T  W  T  F  S
       1  2  3  4  5
 6  7  8  9 10 11 12
13 14 15 16 17 18 19
20 21 22 23 24 25 26
27 28 29 30 31
```

DECEMBER
```
 S  M  T  W  T  F  S
                1  2  3
 4  5  6  7  8  9 10
11 12 13 14 15 16 17
18 19 20 21 22 23 24
25 26 27 28 29 30 31
```

1996

JANUARY
```
 S  M  T  W  T  F  S
    1  2  3  4  5  6
 7  8  9 10 11 12 13
14 15 16 17 18 19 20
21 22 23 24 25 26 27
28 29 30 31
```

FEBRUARY
```
 S  M  T  W  T  F  S
             1  2  3
 4  5  6  7  8  9 10
11 12 13 14 15 16 17
18 19 20 21 22 23 24
25 26 27 28 29
```

MARCH
```
 S  M  T  W  T  F  S
                1  2
 3  4  5  6  7  8  9
10 11 12 13 14 15 16
17 18 19 20 21 22 23
24 25 26 27 28 29 30
31
```

APRIL
```
 S  M  T  W  T  F  S
    1  2  3  4  5  6
 7  8  9 10 11 12 13
14 15 16 17 18 19 20
21 22 23 24 25 26 27
28 29 30
```

MAY
```
 S  M  T  W  T  F  S
          1  2  3  4
 5  6  7  8  9 10 11
12 13 14 15 16 17 18
19 20 21 22 23 24 25
26 27 28 29 30 31
```

JUNE
```
 S  M  T  W  T  F
                1
 2  3  4  5  6  7
 9 10 11 12 13 14
16 17 18 19 20 21
23 24 25 26 27 28
30
```

JULY
```
 S  M  T  W  T  F  S
    1  2  3  4  5  6
 7  8  9 10 11 12 13
14 15 16 17 18 19 20
21 22 23 24 25 26 27
28 29 30 31
```

AUGUST
```
 S  M  T  W  T  F  S
             1  2  3
 4  5  6  7  8  9 10
11 12 13 14 15 16 17
18 19 20 21 22 23 24
25 26 27 28 29 30 31
```

SEPTEMBER
```
 S  M  T  W  T  F  S
 1  2  3  4  5  6  7
 8  9 10 11 12 13 14
15 16 17 18 19 20 21
22 23 24 25 26 27 28
29 30
```

OCTOBER
```
 S  M  T  W  T  F  S
       1  2  3  4  5
 6  7  8  9 10 11 12
13 14 15 16 17 18 19
20 21 22 23 24 25 26
27 28 29 30 31
```

NOVEMBER
```
 S  M  T  W  T  F  S
                1  2
 3  4  5  6  7  8  9
10 11 12 13 14 15 16
17 18 19 20 21 22 23
24 25 26 27 28 29 30
```

DECEMBER
```
 S  M  T  W  T  F
 1  2  3  4  5  6
 8  9 10 11 12 13
15 16 17 18 19 20
22 23 24 25 26 27
29 30 31
```

JANUARY

M	T	W	T	F	S
2	3	4	5	6	7
9	10	11	12	13	14
16	17	18	19	20	21
23	24	25	26	27	28
30	31				

FEBRUARY

S	M	T	W	T	F	S
			1	2	3	4
5	6	7	8	9	10	11
12	13	14	15	16	17	18
19	20	21	22	23	24	25
26	27	28				

MARCH

S	M	T	W	T	F	S
			1	2	3	4
5	6	7	8	9	10	11
12	13	14	15	16	17	18
19	20	21	22	23	24	25
26	27	28	29	30	31	

APRIL

S	M	T	W	T	F	S
						1
2	3	4	5	6	7	8
9	10	11	12	13	14	15
16	17	18	19	20	21	22
23	24	25	26	27	28	29
30						

MAY

M	T	W	T	F	S
1	2	3	4	5	6
8	9	10	11	12	13
15	16	17	18	19	20
22	23	24	25	26	27
29	30	31			

JUNE

S	M	T	W	T	F	S
				1	2	3
4	5	6	7	8	9	10
11	12	13	14	15	16	17
18	19	20	21	22	23	24
25	26	27	28	29	30	

JULY

S	M	T	W	T	F	S
						1
2	3	4	5	6	7	8
9	10	11	12	13	14	15
16	17	18	19	20	21	22
23	24	25	26	27	28	29
30	31					

AUGUST

S	M	T	W	T	F	S
		1	2	3	4	5
6	7	8	9	10	11	12
13	14	15	16	17	18	19
20	21	22	23	24	25	26
27	28	29	30	31		

SEPTEMBER

M	T	W	T	F	S
				1	2
4	5	6	7	8	9
11	12	13	14	15	16
18	19	20	21	22	23
25	26	27	28	29	30

OCTOBER

S	M	T	W	T	F	S
1	2	3	4	5	6	7
8	9	10	11	12	13	14
15	16	17	18	19	20	21
22	23	24	25	26	27	28
29	30	31				

NOVEMBER

S	M	T	W	T	F	S
			1	2	3	4
5	6	7	8	9	10	11
12	13	14	15	16	17	18
19	20	21	22	23	24	25
26	27	28	29	30		

DECEMBER

S	M	T	W	T	F	S
					1	2
3	4	5	6	7	8	9
10	11	12	13	14	15	16
17	18	19	20	21	22	23
24	25	26	27	28	29	30
31						

1995